the steak book

Susanna Tee

p

This is a Parragon Publishing Book
First published in 2005

Parragon Publishing
Queen Street House
4 Queen Street
Bath BA1 1HE
United Kingdom

Produced by The Bridgewater Book Company

Photographer Emma Neish
Home Economist Joy Skipper

ISBN 1-40544-882-2

Printed in China

NOTE This book uses imperial, metric, or US cup measurements. Follow the same units of
measurement throughout; do not mix imperial and metric. All spoon measurements are level:
teaspoons are assumed to be 5 ml, and tablespoons are assumed to be 15 ml. Unless otherwise
stated, milk is assumed to be whole, eggs and individual vegetables such as carrots are medium,
and pepper is freshly ground black pepper. Flour has been measured by dipping the cup into
the flour and leveling the top.

The times given for each recipe are an approximate guide only. The preparation times may
differ according to the techniques used by different people and the cooking times may vary
as a result of the type of oven used. Ovens should be preheated to the specified temperature.
If using a fan-assisted oven, check the manufacturer's instructions for adjusting the time
and temperature.

Recipes using raw eggs should be avoided by infants, the elderly, pregnant women,
convalescents, and anyone suffering from an illness.

contents

America is renowned for its beef, especially its steak, which is hardly surprising since it is the world's largest supplier of grain-fed cattle. Vast herds of beef cattle roam the plains of Texas and the Western Ranges, where they feed first on grass, then on grain, before being brought to market.

Most people, therefore, think of archetypal American food in terms of its enormous pan-fried steaks and barbecued hamburgers, but even in this realm of traditional American fare, there are many different culinary influences at work, out of which have developed steak dishes with Mexican, French, Italian, Russian, Chinese, and Japanese flavors, to name but a few. The recipes in this book encompass the whole range, from the fiery to the fragrant, in such steak specials as Chili con Carne Burritos, Pan-Fried Steaks with Béarnaise Sauce, Italian Steak Heroes, Beef Stroganoff, Teriyaki Kabobs, and Stir-Fried Steak and Broccoli with Noodles. But there are also some great, all-American classics not to be missed,

introduction

including Steak Waldorf Salad, Steak Hash and Sunny-Side-Up Eggs, Surf 'n' Turf Skewers, and Chicken-Fried Steaks.

There are a few essentials when it comes to cooking steak successfully, whatever the cut. Do not season steak with salt before cooking, as this draws out the meat's juices, making it less moist and flavorsome. However, seasoning with pepper is fine. While the steak is cooking, don't be tempted to prod it too much, as this will also allow the precious juices to escape. Use a spatula rather than a fork for turning, for the same reason. Finally, always err on the side of undercooking steak rather than overcooking it, since when you remove the steak from the heat, its internal temperature continues to cook the meat for a few minutes.

With these top tips under your rancher's hat and the recipes to follow, get ready to sink your teeth into some succulent steak in all its glorious guises.

Steak dishes need not be extravagant—in size or in cost. In the recipes in this chapter, you can savor a modest portion of delicious tender steak as a snack or a light meal.

Even the humble sandwich is elevated to a quality eating experience with steak as its central ingredient, and here are some prime examples, from the pure and simple Mustard Steak Sandwich, with the addition of pan-fried onions, to Italian Steak Heroes—a feast of Bolognese sauce topped with mozzarella cheese, all in a ciabatta roll. Steak also features in salad, for a healthy option—in a variation on the classic Waldorf Salad and in the refreshingly fruity Asian Steak and Orange Salad.

on the light side

prepare 15 minutes
cook 6–10 minutes *serves* 4

This salad is traditionally a combination of celery, apples, and walnuts, dressed with mayonnaise. Here, with the addition of sliced steak, it is turned into a light lunch or supper dish.

steak waldorf salad

ingredients

2 tenderloin steaks, about 6 oz/175 g
   each and 1 inch/2.5 cm thick
olive or sunflower-seed oil, for brushing
1 tbsp wholegrain mustard
⅔ cup mayonnaise
1 tbsp lemon juice

1 lb 2 oz/500 g eating apples
4 celery stalks, thinly sliced
½ cup walnut halves, broken into pieces
3½ oz/100 g mixed salad greens
pepper

one Heat a thick, cast-iron stove-top pan or heavy-bottom skillet over medium heat. Brush each steak with oil and season to taste with pepper. When the pan is hot, add the steaks to the pan and cook for 6–7 minutes for rare or 8–10 minutes for medium, turning the steaks frequently and brushing once or twice with oil. Remove from the pan and set aside.

two Meanwhile, stir the mustard into the mayonnaise. Put the lemon juice into a large bowl. Peel and core the apples, then cut them into small chunks and immediately toss in the lemon juice. Stir in the mustard mayonnaise. Add the celery and walnuts to the apple mixture and toss together.

three Arrange the salad greens on 4 plates, then divide the apple mixture between them. Very thinly slice the steaks, arrange on top of the salad, and serve at once.

did you know?

Waldorf Salad is named after the prestigious Waldorf Astoria Hotel in New York, as it was here that the dish originated at the end of the 19th century.

prepare 20 minutes, plus 3–4 hours' marinating
cook 10–14 minutes *serves* 4

The combination of the Asian flavors of soy sauce and ginger, which are used to flavor the steak, and the oranges in the accompanying salad complement each other well and make this a refreshing summer dish.

asian steak and orange salad

ingredients

4 tbsp soy sauce

4 tbsp red wine

2-inch/5-cm piece fresh gingerroot, grated

2 garlic cloves, crushed

1 lb 9 oz/700 g sirloin or rump steak, about 1½ inches/4 cm thick

olive or sunflower-seed oil, for oiling

3 oranges

2 tbsp white wine vinegar

5 tbsp extra virgin olive oil

1 tbsp chopped fresh flat-leaf parsley

6½ oz/180 g mixed salad greens

1 small onion, very thinly sliced

salt and pepper

one To make the marinade, put the soy sauce, wine, ginger, and garlic into a large, shallow, nonmetallic dish large enough to hold the steak, and mix together. Add the steak and turn in the marinade to coat it. Cover and let marinate in the refrigerator for 3–4 hours, turning occasionally.

two When ready to cook, preheat the broiler or barbecue. Using a slotted spoon, remove the steak from the marinade, put onto an oiled broiler or rack, and cook under or over medium heat for 10 minutes for rare or 12–14 minutes for medium, turning the steak frequently and basting once or twice with the marinade. Set aside to cool slightly.

three Meanwhile, squeeze the juice from 1 of the oranges and put into a bowl. Add the vinegar, oil, parsley, and salt and pepper to taste to the orange juice and whisk together. Peel and thinly slice the remaining oranges.

four Arrange the salad greens on 4 plates, then divide the orange and onion slices between them. Very thinly slice the steak and arrange on top. Whisk the salad dressing again and drizzle over the salad before serving.

variation and serving recommendation

Although steak is the traditional meat to use in this popular salad, pork tenderloin also combines well with the oranges. Marinate and broil pork tenderloins until thoroughly cooked, then thinly slice. Serve the salad with some crusty bread.

prepare 15 minutes, plus 1 hour's standing
cook 20–25 minutes *serves* 4

Introduced by the Italians and packed with delicious Italian ingredients, this recipe uses Bolognese sauce. Wrap the sandwiches in foil for transporting and supply lots of paper napkins for catching the juices!

italian steak heroes

ingredients

1 tbsp olive oil
1 small onion, finely chopped
1 garlic clove, finely chopped
1 small red bell pepper, finely chopped
3½ oz/100 g white mushrooms, finely chopped
⅞ cup fresh ground steak
½ cup red wine

2 tbsp tomato paste
4 ciabatta rolls
extra virgin olive oil, for brushing
2¾ oz/75 g mozzarella cheese
2 tbsp torn fresh basil leaves, plus extra basil leaves, to garnish
salt and pepper

one Heat the olive oil in a large pan over medium heat, add the onion, garlic, red bell pepper, and mushrooms, and cook, stirring occasionally, for 5–10 minutes until softened and beginning to brown.

two Add the ground steak and cook, stirring frequently and breaking up any lumps with a wooden spoon, for 5 minutes until browned on all sides. Add the wine, tomato paste, and salt and pepper to taste and let simmer for 10 minutes, stirring occasionally. Remove from the heat.

three Split the bread rolls in half and brush both halves with extra virgin olive oil. Put the bottom halves onto a piece of foil and spoon an equal quantity of the sauce on top of each.

four Slice the cheese, then divide between the roll bottoms and arrange on top of the sauce. Add the torn basil leaves and cover with the tops of the rolls. Press down gently and wrap in the foil. Leave the sandwiches for at least 1 hour before serving, garnished with basil leaves.

did you know?

This classic sandwich comes under a variety of labels—the hoagie, the submarine, the bomber, the grinder, the wedge, and the zep, to name but a few!

prepare 15 minutes, plus 2 hours' freezing
cook 15–22 minutes *serves* 4

The steak in this recipe should be cut into very thin slices, so it is partially frozen beforehand to make this easier to do. Put the steak in the freezer for about 2 hours before you need it.

philly cheesesteak

ingredients

1 baguette

12 oz/350 g boneless rib-eye steak, partially frozen

3 tbsp olive oil

1 onion, thinly sliced

1 green bell pepper, thinly sliced

2¾ oz/75 g provolone or mozzarella cheese, thinly sliced

salt and pepper

hot pepper sauce, to serve

one Cut the bread into 4 equal lengths, then cut each piece horizontally in half. Thinly slice the partially frozen steak across the grain.

two Heat 2 tablespoons of the oil in a large skillet over medium heat, add the onion and green bell pepper, and cook, stirring occasionally, for 10–15 minutes until softened and golden brown. Push the mixture to one side of the skillet.

three Heat the remaining oil in the skillet over medium heat. When hot, add the steak, and stir-fry for 4–5 minutes until tender. Stir the onion mixture and steak together and season to taste with salt and pepper.

four Preheat the broiler to medium. Divide the steak mixture between the 4 bottom halves of bread and top with the cheese. Broil for 1–2 minutes until the cheese has melted, then cover with the top halves of bread and press down gently. Serve at once with hot pepper sauce.

did you know?

These sandwiches originated from the Italians in South Philadelphia, in 1930, where they used chicken or steak. They say that you cannot make a true Philly Cheesesteak outside Philadelphia, as the authentic variety of bread roll is unavailable elsewhere. As a compromise, this recipe uses a baguette instead.

prepare 15 minutes
cook 20–30 minutes   *serves* 4

A real steak sandwich, filled with prime steak, is a treat, but don't be tempted to use a cheap cut, as there is nothing worse than trying to eat a tough, chewy piece of meat between two pieces of crusty bread!

mustard steak sandwich

ingredients

1 baguette
butter, for spreading
mixed salad greens
3 tbsp olive oil
2 onions, thinly sliced

1 lb 8 oz/675 g rump or sirloin steak,
   about 1 inch/2.5 cm thick
1 tbsp Worcestershire sauce
2 tbsp whole grain mustard
2 tbsp water
salt and pepper

one Cut the bread into 4 equal lengths, then cut each piece horizontally in half. Spread each half with some butter and add a few salad greens to the bottom halves.

two Heat 2 tablespoons of the oil in a large, heavy-bottom skillet over medium heat. Add the onions and cook, stirring occasionally, for 10–15 minutes until softened and golden brown. Using a slotted spoon, transfer to a plate and set aside.

three Increase the heat to high and add the remaining oil to the skillet. When hot, add the steak, season to taste with pepper, and cook quickly on both sides to seal. Reduce the heat to medium and cook, turning once, for 2½–3 minutes each side for rare or 3½–5 minutes each side for medium. Transfer the steak to the plate with the onions.

four Add the Worcestershire sauce, mustard, and water to the skillet and stir to deglaze by scraping any sediment from the bottom of the skillet. Return the onions to the skillet, season to taste with salt and pepper, and mix well.

five Thinly slice the steak across the grain, divide it between the 4 bottom halves of bread, and cover with the onion mixture. Cover with the top halves of bread and press down gently. Serve at once.

variation

If preferred, the bread can be toasted, either before being filled or after being filled, on both sides or just the outer sides—the choice is yours!

prepare 15 minutes
cook 45–50 minutes makes 8

on the light side 19

Whether this recipe is American or Mexican is debatable. Either way, popular varieties of this spicy dish exist in all regions of America, but whatever the recipe, it is especially good when made with freshly ground steak.

chili con carne burritos

ingredients

1 tbsp sunflower-seed oil, plus extra
  for oiling
1 onion, finely chopped
1 garlic clove, finely chopped
1–2 tsp chili powder, to taste
1 tsp ground cumin
½ tsp paprika
1 lb 2 oz/500 g fresh ground steak
14 oz/400 g canned chopped tomatoes

2 tbsp tomato paste
½ tsp dried oregano
14 oz/400 g canned red kidney beans,
  drained
8 wheat tortillas
3½ oz/100 g Cheddar cheese, grated
salt and pepper
fresh cilantro sprigs, to garnish
guacamole or Tomato Salsa, to serve

one Preheat the oven to 350°F/180°C. Oil a large, shallow ovenproof dish.

two Heat the oil in a large pan over medium heat, add the onion and garlic, and cook, stirring occasionally, for 10 minutes, or until softened and beginning to brown. Add the chili powder, cumin, and paprika and cook, stirring constantly, for 1 minute.

three Add the ground steak and cook, stirring frequently and breaking up any lumps with a wooden spoon, for 5 minutes, or until browned all over. Add the tomatoes with their juice, tomato paste, and oregano and let simmer, uncovered, for 10 minutes, stirring occasionally. Stir in the beans during the last 2–3 minutes of cooking. Season to taste with salt and pepper.

four Meanwhile, warm the tortillas according to the instructions provided on the package.

five Divide the meat mixture between the tortillas, spooning it down the center of each. Fold in the sides of each tortilla, overlapping the edges, then fold in the remaining edges to form a neat package. Place in the prepared dish, seam-sides down, and sprinkle over the cheese.

six Cover the dish with foil and bake in the oven for 20 minutes, or until piping hot. Serve at once, with guacamole or Tomato Salsa generously spooned over each burrito and garnished with cilantro sprigs.

prepare 15 minutes, plus 6–8 hours' marinating
cook 5–10 minutes   *serves* 4

In Texas and Mexico, the steak for this recipe would be cooked over charcoal. You can do this too, although using the broiler may be more convenient if the sun isn't shining!

grilled steak fajitas

ingredients

2 tbsp sunflower-seed oil, plus extra for
  oiling
finely grated rind of 1 lime
1 tbsp lime juice
2 garlic cloves, crushed
¼ tsp ground coriander
¼ tsp ground cumin
pinch of sugar
1 piece of rump steak, about 1 lb 8 oz/
  675 g and ¾ inch/2 cm thick

4 wheat tortillas
1 avocado
2 tomatoes, thinly sliced
4 tbsp sour cream
4 scallions, thinly sliced
salt and pepper

To garnish
cilantro sprigs
lime wedges

one To make the marinade, put the oil, lime rind and juice, garlic, coriander, cumin, sugar, and salt and pepper to taste into a large, shallow, nonmetallic dish large enough to hold the steak and mix together. Add the steak and turn in the marinade to coat it. Cover and let marinate in the refrigerator for 6–8 hours or up to 24 hours, turning occasionally.

two When ready to cook, preheat the broiler or barbecue. Using a slotted spoon, remove the steak from the marinade, put onto an oiled broiler or grill rack, and cook under or over medium heat for 5 minutes for rare or 8–10 minutes for medium, turning the steak frequently and basting once or twice with any remaining marinade.

three Meanwhile, warm the tortillas according to the instructions on the package. Peel, pit, and slice the avocado.

four Thinly slice the steak across the grain and arrange an equal quantity of the slices on one side of each tortilla. Add the tomato and avocado slices, top with a spoonful of sour cream, and sprinkle over the scallions. Fold over and eat at once.

did you know?

Fajitas originated in Mexico and were brought across the border into Texas. It was the Texans who made them popular and they are now eaten in restaurants serving Tex-Mex food all over America. Fajita is Spanish for "skirt steak," which is a cut that you could use, but flank or, better still, rump is more tender.

prepare 10 minutes, plus 3–4 hours' marinating
cook 8–10 minutes *serves* 4

These filled tortillas make the ideal fast-food snack—but a healthy one! The combination of fresh lime juice and chili is an authentic Mexican flavoring now widely popular in America. Omit the chili if your taste buds prefer something milder.

steak and lime tortillas

ingredients

2 rump steaks, about 8 oz/225 g each
finely grated rind and juice of 1 lime
1 fresh green chili, seeded and finely
  chopped
2 garlic cloves, crushed
pinch of sugar
2 tbsp olive oil
1 small onion, thinly sliced

1 red bell pepper, thinly sliced
4 wheat tortillas
salt and pepper
cilantro sprigs, to garnish

To serve
Tomato Salsa
sour cream

one Thinly slice the steaks. To make the marinade, put the lime rind and juice, chili, garlic, sugar, and salt and pepper to taste into a large, shallow, nonmetallic dish and mix together. Add the steak and turn in the marinade to coat it. Cover and let marinate in the refrigerator for 3–4 hours, turning occasionally.

two Heat the oil in a large skillet over medium heat. Add the onion and red bell pepper and cook, stirring frequently, for 5 minutes until softened. Using a slotted spoon, remove the steak from the marinade, add to the skillet, and cook, stirring constantly, for 2–3 minutes until browned. Add the marinade, bring to a boil, and toss together.

three Meanwhile, warm the tortillas according to the instructions on the package. Divide the steak mixture between the tortillas, then fold in one side and roll up each tortilla to form an open-ended container. Serve hot garnished with cilantro sprigs, with Tomato Salsa and sour cream to spoon on top.

did you know?
Tortillas are a round, flat, unleavened bread made from either wheat or cornmeal flour (masa harina). Wheat tortillas are usually larger than corn tortillas, but they are interchangeable in recipes and the choice depends purely on your taste.

prepare about 15 minutes
cook about 20 minutes   *serves* 4–6

You can buy fresh ground steak, but if you want to grind it yourself, rump steak would be the best cut to use for this recipe for both its flavor and tenderness.

steak hash with sunny-side-up eggs

ingredients

1 lb 2 oz/500 g fresh ground steak
1 onion, finely chopped
2 garlic cloves, crushed
1 tbsp red wine vinegar
1 lb 2 oz/500 g potatoes, peeled and
  finely diced

3 tbsp sunflower-seed oil, plus extra for
  pan-frying
a little butter, for pan-frying
4–6 eggs
salt and pepper
fresh watercress sprigs, to garnish
hot pepper sauce, to serve (optional)

one Put the steak into a large bowl and add the onion, garlic, vinegar, potatoes, and salt and pepper to taste. Mix well together.

two Heat the 3 tablespoons of oil in a large, heavy-bottom skillet over high heat. Add the steak mixture and cook, stirring constantly, for 5 minutes, or until browned on all sides. Reduce the heat to medium and, using a spatula, press the mixture into the bottom of the skillet. Cook for an additional 15 minutes, or until the base is well browned and the potatoes are tender. Do not be tempted to stir the hash while it is cooking.

three Just before the end of cooking, heat a generous film of oil in a separate large, heavy-bottom skillet with a lid over medium heat. When hot, add a tablespoon of butter, and, as soon as it has melted, break in the eggs, either a few at a time or all together, depending upon the size of your skillet. Cover and cook for 4–6 minutes until the egg whites have set and the yolks are beginning to set around the edges.

four Cut the hash into 4–6 wedges. Invert each wedge onto a warmed plate, top with a fried egg, and serve at once garnished with watercress and a few drops of hot pepper sauce, if wished.

variations

Corned Beef Hash from New England is a popular variation on this recipe—simply substitute cubed cooked corned beef for the steak. Red Flannel Hash is Corned Beef Hash with the addition of two cooked and cubed beets, and it is these that give the recipe its unusual name.

prepare 20 minutes
cook no cooking   *serves* 4

This traditional, rather old-fashioned, sophisticated dish of raw steak and egg yolk is still served in high-class American restaurants. It can easily be made at home, but read the Cook's Tip for advice on preparing it.

steak tartare

ingredients

1 lb 2 oz/500 g tenderloin steak
1 small onion or shallot, very finely
   chopped
8 tbsp chopped fresh parsley
4 tbsp capers, rinsed and drained
1¾ oz/50 g canned anchovy fillets,
   drained and finely chopped
4 eggs
salt and pepper

To serve
crisp mixed salad
hot pepper sauce
freshly squeezed lemon juice
Worcestershire sauce
French mustard

one Prepare the steak immediately before serving. Cut away any fat or membrane and, using a sharp knife, grind or very finely chop the steak. Alternatively, use a food processor, but it is important not to overprocess the steak into a pulp. Process the steak in short bursts and keep scraping down the sides of the bowl.

two Transfer the steak to a bowl, add the onion, parsley, and salt and pepper to taste, and mix well together. Spoon the mixture onto chilled plates and form into a mound, then make an indentation in the center of each.

three Arrange small piles of the capers and anchovies around the mounds. Break the eggs, one at a time, separating the yolks from the egg whites, and place the egg yolks in the hollows of the steak mounds. (The egg whites can be used in another dish.)

four Serve at once, with a crisp mixed salad and accompanied by hot pepper sauce, lemon juice, Worcestershire sauce, and French mustard, so that each person can season the Steak Tartare according to their taste.

cook's tip

This dish, which contains raw eggs, should not be served to infants, the elderly, pregnant women, convalescents, and anyone suffering from an illness. It is essential that the eggs and steak are very fresh, and the steak should be ground at home to avoid contamination.

prepare 10–20 minutes
cook 6–12 minutes *serves* 4

Nothing beats a burger made with steak. If you prefer, you can grind the steak at home, and rump steak, including its fat, is a good cut to use. Real burgers, incidentally, do not use egg to bind the mixture.

the best
steak burgers

ingredients

1 lb 2 oz/500 g rump steak or fresh
   ground steak
½ small onion, very finely chopped or
   grated (optional)
vegetable oil, for broiling or pan-frying
salt and pepper
4 hamburger buns

To garnish
lettuce leaves
sliced gherkins (optional)

To serve
tomato ketchup, hot pepper sauce,
   Homemade Tomato Sauce, Roasted
   Bell Pepper Relish, Tomato Salsa,
   or mustard

one If you have chosen to grind the steak at home, using a sharp knife, very finely chop or grind the steak. Alternatively, use a food processor, but it is important not to overprocess the steak to a pulp. Process the steak in short bursts and keep scraping down the sides of the bowl.

two Transfer the steak to a bowl, add the onion, if using, and salt and pepper, and mix well together. Divide the mixture into 4 portions and shape each into a flat, round patty, about 1 inch/2.5 cm thick.

three Broil or pan-fry the burgers according to your preference. To broil, preheat the broiler to medium-high and brush both sides of the burgers with oil. To pan-fry, heat a film of oil in the bottom of a large, heavy-bottom skillet over medium-high heat. Cook the burgers, turning once, for 6–12 minutes until browned and cooked according to your taste.

four Meanwhile, split the hamburger buns in half, line with lettuce leaves, and add some gherkins, if wished. Put a cooked burger inside each bun and serve at once, with the accompaniments of your choice.

did you know?

It is said that the burger, hamburger, or beefburger gets its name from the city of Hamburg in Germany, where it originated, and not, as some might think, from the fact that it is made from ham or beef. The Germans introduced it to America, where it was quickly adopted.

Only the weather need dictate which direct-heat method you choose for preparing these recipes, from the colorful Tender Steak and Vegetable Kabobs to the sumptuous Tenderloin Steak with Bleu Cheese Sauce.

Cooking over charcoal requires more preparation time—allow about 45 minutes before cooking for the flames to die down, leaving the coals glowing red. During cooking, keep the steak well brushed with oil and, if the food is in danger of overdoing, move the rack up farther away from the heat. But broiling also needs some forethought—preheat the broiler on high heat for 5–10 minutes with the broiler pan underneath for the perfect broiled steak.

under the broiler or over the grill

prepare 5 minutes
cook 5–20 minutes *serves* any number

This is undoubtedly the steak recipe that you will turn to time and time again, and even if you don't have a broiler or grill, all is not lost. Using a thick, cast-iron stove-top grill pan or griddle instead, preheat it and cook the steaks as in the recipe.

the perfect broiled steak

ingredients

rump, sirloin, or tenderloin steaks,
  about 6–8 oz/175–225 g each
olive or sunflower-seed oil, for brushing
  and oiling
pepper

To serve
Maître d'Hôtel Butter
jacket baked potatoes
green salad

one Preheat the broiler or barbecue. Brush each steak with oil and season to taste with pepper.

two Put each steak onto an oiled broiler or grill rack and cook under or over a medium heat for the required length of time and according to your taste: for ¾-inch/2-cm thick steaks, 5 minutes for rare, 8–10 minutes for medium, and 12–14 minutes for well done; for 1-inch/2.5-cm thick steaks, 6–7 minutes for rare, 8–10 minutes for medium, and 12–15 minutes for well done; for 1½-inch/4-cm thick steaks, 10 minutes for rare, 12–14 minutes for medium, and 18–20 minutes for well done. During cooking, turn the steaks frequently, using a spatula rather than a sharp tool so that you don't pierce the meat and allow the juices to escape. When you turn the steaks, brush them once or twice with oil. Watch the steaks constantly during cooking to ensure that they don't get too brown.

three Serve each perfectly broiled steak at once, topped with a slice of Maître d'Hôtel Butter and accompanied by a jacket baked potato and green salad.

cook's tip

If the steaks have a piece of fat running along them, cut or snip into it at regular intervals to prevent the steaks from curling during cooking. A jacket baked potato has been suggested as a healthy accompaniment to the steaks, but you could serve them with French Fries and Crispy Onion Rings instead.

prepare 10 minutes, plus 6–8 hours' marinating
cook 12–18 minutes *serves* 4

Marinating steak helps to tenderize it and it is therefore an ideal approach for tougher cuts of steak. In fact, the marinade benefits the steak all round, since the longer it is marinated, the more flavor it will have.

marinated broiled flank steak

ingredients

1 piece flank steak, about 1 lb 8 oz–
  2 lb/675–900 g

½ cup red wine

3 tbsp olive or sunflower-seed oil, plus
  extra for oiling

3 tbsp Worcestershire or soy sauce

2 garlic cloves, crushed

salt and pepper

fresh watercress sprigs, to garnish

one Prick the steak all over on both sides with a fork to ensure that the marinade will penetrate the meat. To make the marinade, put the wine, oil, Worcestershire sauce, garlic, and salt and pepper to taste into a large, shallow, nonmetallic dish large enough to hold the steak, and mix together. Add the steak and turn in the marinade to coat it. Cover and let marinate in the refrigerator for 6–8 hours or up to 24 hours, turning the steak occasionally.

two When ready to cook, preheat the broiler or barbecue. Using a slotted spoon, remove the steak from the marinade, put onto an oiled broiler or grill rack, and cook under or over medium heat for 12–18 minutes, depending on the thickness of the steak and according to your taste, turning frequently and basting with the marinade.

three Transfer the steak to a warmed serving dish and let rest for 5 minutes. To serve, carve the steak thickly across the grain and garnish with watercress sprigs.

did you know?

In Britain, this recipe is called Flank Steak but in fact uses rump steak—flank in Britain is not the same cut as in America. American flank is a boneless, narrow, tender cut suitable for pan-frying, broiling, and grilling. British flank is better suited to stewing, although thickly-sliced flank can be pan-fried.

prepare 10 minutes, plus 3 hours' marinating
cook 10–15 minutes   *serves* 6

This popular dish from California is perfect for cooking over a barbecue, and although you could cook the steak whole, it is much more fun and attractive to serve it on skewers.

teriyaki kabobs

ingredients

2 lb/900 g rump steak, about 1 inch/
  2.5 cm thick

12 bay leaves

4 tbsp soy sauce

2 tbsp vegetable oil, plus extra for oiling

2 tbsp sake

2 tbsp mirin

scant ¼ cup sugar

1 garlic clove, crushed

1-inch/2.5-cm piece fresh gingerroot,
  grated

To serve

noodles

freshly cooked vegetables

lemon wedges

one Cut the steak into 1-inch/2.5-cm cubes. Thread the steak cubes onto 12 oiled flat metal kabob skewers, leaving a small space between each cube so that the steak cooks evenly. Add a bay leaf to each skewer.

two To make the marinade, put all the remaining ingredients into a large, shallow, nonmetallic dish large enough to hold the kabobs, and mix together. Add the kabobs and turn them in the marinade to coat them. Cover and let marinate in the refrigerator for at least 3 hours or up to 12 hours, turning occasionally.

three When ready to cook, preheat the broiler or barbecue. Remove the kabobs from the marinade, put onto an oiled broiler or grill rack, and cook under or over medium heat for 10–15 minutes until the meat is tender and according to your taste, turning frequently and basting with the marinade—this is particularly important toward the end of cooking so that the kabobs brown but do not burn. Serve with lemon wedges, freshly cooked vegetables, and noodles.

variations

Teriyaki literally translated means "gloss grilled," and in Japan, from where it originates, teriyaki is used as either a marinade or a sauce. There, it is a particularly popular way of cooking tuna steaks, but you could also try it with other fish steaks such as salmon and swordfish, as well as with chicken.

prepare 15 minutes, plus 2–4 hours' marinating
cook 7–12 minutes *serves* 4

Using tender cuts of steak, this dish is simplicity itself. Steak and vegetables, threaded and served together on skewers, need only an accompaniment of rice, basil sprigs, and lemon wedges, although a dip or sauce would add a finishing touch. The Steak Dipping Sauces are particularly good.

tender steak and vegetable kabobs

ingredients

1 lb 8 oz/675 g sirloin or tenderloin
  steak
2 tbsp olive oil, plus extra for oiling
1 tbsp red wine vinegar
4 tbsp red wine
1 tbsp French mustard
1 garlic clove, crushed
2 red or green bell peppers

2 zucchini
8 pearl onions
salt and pepper

To serve
rice
fresh basil sprigs
lemon wedges

one Cut the steak into 1½-inch/4-cm cubes. To make the marinade, put the oil, vinegar, wine, mustard, garlic, and salt and pepper to taste into a large, nonmetallic bowl, and mix together. Add the steak cubes and turn in the marinade to coat them. Cover and let marinate in the refrigerator for 2–4 hours or up to 24 hours, turning occasionally.

two When you are ready to cook, preheat the broiler or barbecue. Core, seed, and cut the bell peppers into 1¼-inch/3-cm pieces. Cut the zucchini into 1-inch/2.5-cm pieces. Using a slotted spoon, remove the steak from the marinade. Thread an equal number of the steak cubes, bell peppers, and zucchini alternately, with the onion in the center, onto 8 oiled flat metal kabob skewers or presoaked wooden skewers.

three Put the kabobs onto an oiled broiler or grill rack and cook under or over medium heat for 7–12 minutes until tender and slightly charred, or according to your taste, turning frequently and basting with the marinade. Serve hot on the skewers with rice, basil sprigs, and lemon wedges.

cook's tip
If you are using metal kabob skewers, they simply need oiling before use, but if you are using wooden ones, presoak them in cold water for 30 minutes. This helps to stop them from burning during cooking.

prepare 20 minutes
cook 4–8 minutes *serves* 2

Tenderloin steak is, of all the cuts, the most expensive, but this is because it is the most tender, and it perfectly complements the shrimp in this recipe. This is a dish for entertaining in style!

surf 'n' turf skewers

ingredients

8 oz/225 g tenderloin steak, about
 1 inch/2.5 cm thick

8 raw jumbo shrimp, in their shells

olive oil, for oiling

4 tbsp butter

2 garlic cloves, crushed

3 tbsp chopped fresh parsley, plus extra
 parsley sprigs, to garnish

finely grated rind and juice of 1 lime

salt and pepper

lime wedges, to garnish

crusty bread, to serve

one Cut the steak into 1-inch/2.5-cm cubes. To prepare the shrimp, pull off their heads with your fingers, then peel off their shells, leaving the tails on. Using a sharp knife, make a shallow slit along the underside of each shrimp, then pull out the dark vein and discard. Rinse the shrimp under cold running water and dry well on paper towels.

two Thread an equal number of the steak cubes and shrimp onto 4 oiled flat metal kabob skewers or presoaked wooden skewers. Season the kabobs to taste with pepper.

three Preheat the broiler to high. Meanwhile, put the butter and garlic into a small pan and heat gently until melted. Remove from the heat and add the parsley, lime rind and juice, and salt and pepper to taste. Leave in a warm place so that the butter remains melted.

four Brush the kabobs with a little of the melted butter. Put the kabobs onto an oiled broiler or grill rack and cook under or over medium heat for 4–8 minutes until the steak is cooked according to your taste and the shrimp turn pink, turning the kabobs frequently during cooking, and brushing with the remaining melted butter.

five Serve the kabobs hot on the skewers, with the remaining butter spooned over. Garnish with lime wedges and parsley sprigs and serve with crusty bread to mop up the buttery juices.

variations

Recipes for Surf 'n' Turf, otherwise known as Sea and Shore, vary widely in different regions of America. Broiled or grilled steak and lobster is the most well-known pairing, but the surf can be crab, shrimp (as it is here) or scallops, and the turf can even be chicken.

Tender steaks are topped with a crisp crust of fiery-flavored buttery crumbs. Not only do they add flavor, they also help to lock in the steaks' natural juices in the last few minutes of cooking.

deviled
sirloin steaks

ingredients

4 tbsp butter

1 tbsp mustard powder

1 tbsp Worcestershire sauce

olive or vegetable oil, for oiling

4 sirloin steaks, about 6–8 oz/175–225 g
    each and 1½ inches/4 cm thick

¾ cup day-old white bread crumbs

salt and pepper

freshly cooked vegetables, to serve

one Preheat the broiler to medium. Meanwhile, put the butter into a small bowl and beat with a wooden spoon until softened. Add the mustard powder, Worcestershire sauce, and salt and pepper to taste and blend together. Set the mixture aside.

two Put the steaks onto an oiled broiler rack and cook under the broiler for 8 minutes for rare, 10–12 minutes for medium, or 16–18 minutes for well done, turning frequently. Remove the broiler pan from the heat and place on a heatproof surface.

three Spread the deviled butter mixture on top of the steaks, then sprinkle over the bread crumbs, pressing them down well. Return the broiler pan to the broiler and cook for an additional 2–3 minutes until the bread crumbs are golden brown. Serve at once with freshly cooked vegetables.

variation

The word deviled in culinary terms means to cook a food with hot spices or condiments—mustard and Worcestershire sauce in this case. Should you wish to make the butter more deviled, you could add a pinch of cayenne pepper, a few drops of hot pepper sauce, or a pinch of curry powder.

prepare 10 minutes, plus 4 hours' marinating
cook 8–12 minutes *serves* 4

Thick chimichurri sauce, which originates from Argentina, where it is eaten with gusto, is slightly hot and packed with herbs, but, most notably, it is a sauce for garlic lovers!

steak with chimichurri sauce

ingredients

1 small onion, quartered

4 garlic cloves, peeled

¾ oz/20 g fresh parsley

2 tbsp fresh oregano leaves

generous ⅓ cup olive oil, plus extra for oiling

2 tbsp red wine vinegar

¼ tsp cayenne pepper

4 rump steaks, about 6–8 oz/175–225 g each and ¾ inch/2 cm thick

salt and pepper

mixed salad, to serve

one To make the chimichurri sauce, put the onion and garlic into a food processor and pulse until finely chopped, scraping down the sides of the bowl with a spatula once or twice. Add the parsley and oregano and pulse again until chopped. Pour in the oil and process to form a smooth purée. Add the vinegar, cayenne pepper, and salt and pepper to taste and mix well.

two Put 12 tablespoons of the sauce into a large, shallow, nonmetallic dish large enough to hold the steaks. Put the remaining sauce into a screw-top jar or airtight container and store in the refrigerator until ready to serve.

three Add the steaks to the dish and turn in the sauce to coat them. Cover and let marinate in the refrigerator for at least 4 hours or up to 24 hours, turning occasionally.

four When ready to cook, preheat the broiler or barbecue. Using a slotted spoon, remove the steak from the marinade, put onto an oiled broiler or grill rack, and cook under or over medium heat for 8–12 minutes, depending on the thickness of the steak and according to your taste, turning frequently and basting with the marinade.

five Serve the steaks with their cooking juices, a mixed salad, and a spoonful of the reserved chimichurri sauce on the side.

cook's tip

The sauce can be made in advance and stored in an airtight container in the refrigerator for 2–3 days. Although traditionally served as a sauce with steak, especially in South America, chimichurri sauce is also good spooned on top of baked, broiled, or grilled fish, or added to tomato soup.

prepare 10 minutes
cook 17–23 minutes　*serves* 4

This recipe in its various forms—some methods marinate the steak and some don't—first appeared in print in 1946 and has been popular ever since.

london broil

ingredients

1 piece of flank steak, about 1 lb 8 oz/
675 g and at least 1 inch/2.5 cm thick
1 garlic clove, halved
1 tsp dried oregano
olive or vegetable oil, for oiling
and brushing

4 tomatoes, halved
8 portobello mushrooms
salt and pepper
fresh rosemary sprigs, to garnish
freshly cooked vegetables, to serve

one Preheat the broiler to high. Using a sharp knife, score the steak in a diamond pattern on both sides. Rub each side of the steak with the garlic, then sprinkle over the oregano and season to taste with salt and pepper.

two Put the steak onto an oiled broiler rack and cook under the broiler for 12–18 minutes, depending on the thickness of the steak and according to your taste. Transfer to a warmed serving dish and let rest for 5 minutes.

three Meanwhile, brush the tomatoes and mushrooms generously with oil and season to taste with salt and pepper. Arrange the tomatoes cut-side up and the mushrooms underside uppermost on the broiler rack and broil for 5 minutes, or until cooked, turning the mushrooms once and brushing with more oil.

four Thinly carve the steak at an angle across the grain and serve with the tomatoes and mushrooms and freshly cooked vegetables.

did you know?

The name London Broil refers to the style of cooking, not the cut of steak, as some people think. You even see recipes that list "1 London Broil" in the list of ingredients! In Britain they traditionally use a piece of rump steak, but in America a larger cut of steak is used, such as flank.

prepare 20 minutes
cook 15–20 minutes   *serves* 6

Medallions of steak, flecked with parsley, wrapped in bacon for added flavor, and served on rounds of toast, are not only delicious but also look very appealing. Surprisingly simple to prepare, they make the perfect dish for entertaining.

steak tournedos

ingredients

8 thin lean bacon slices

olive or vegetable oil, for oiling

1 piece of thin rump steak, about
  1 lb 8 oz/675 g

1 garlic clove, crushed

2 tbsp chopped fresh parsley

6 slices white bread

4 tbsp butter

pepper

fresh thyme sprigs, to garnish

one Preheat the broiler to medium. Put the bacon slices onto an oiled broiler rack and cook for 3 minutes, or until just tender but not crisp, turning once. Drain on paper towels and let cool.

two Meanwhile, trim the fat from the steak. Using a meat mallet or heavy wooden rolling pin, pound it on a wooden board until it is ¼ inch/5 mm thick.

three Lay the bacon slices side-by-side on the wooden board, and then lay the steak on top. Spread the garlic over the steak, then sprinkle over the parsley and season to taste with pepper. Roll the bacon and steak up from one short end to the other, like a jelly roll. Secure with toothpicks at 1-inch/2.5-cm intervals, then cut into 6 x 1-inch/2.5-cm thick slices.

four Put the tournedos onto the broiler rack and cook for 10 minutes, or according to your taste, turning frequently.

five Meanwhile, using a round 4-inch/10-cm cutter or small saucer, cut the bread slices into circles slightly larger than the tournedos.

six When cooked, transfer the tournedos to a warmed plate and let rest while you prepare the toast. Toast the bread circles under the broiler until golden brown on both sides. Meanwhile, melt the butter in a small pan.

seven To serve, put the circles of toast onto warmed serving plates. Remove the toothpicks from the tournedos, place on top of the toast, and pour over the melted butter. Serve at once, garnished with chopped thyme.

did you know?

A tournedos is actually a small, round steak, weighing about 3 oz/85 g and cut about 1 inch/2.5 cm thick, taken from the center of a fillet of beef. The traditional French presentation of tournedos is for them to be barded (covered with a bacon slice) and tied.

This is a decadent dish for lovers of bleu cheese. Serve it when entertaining or you could use individual sirloin or rump steaks as an alternative to the whole tenderloin when serving as a family meal.

tenderloin steak with bleu cheese sauce

ingredients

1 beef tenderloin, about 3 lb/1.3 kg
5 tbsp butter
olive or vegetable oil, for oiling
4½ oz/125 g bleu cheese, crumbled
  (see Cook's Tip)
1 shallot, very finely chopped

generous ⅓ cup Madeira or dry sherry
⅔ cup heavy cream
salt and pepper
chopped fresh parsley, to garnish
freshly cooked green beans, to serve

one Preheat the broiler or barbecue. Tie the tenderloin widthwise at regular intervals with string to form a neat shape. Put the butter into a small bowl and beat with a wooden spoon until softened. Spread 2 tablespoons of the softened butter evenly all over the tenderloin. Season to taste with pepper.

two Put the tenderloin onto an oiled broiler or grill rack and cook under or over high heat, turning frequently, until browned on all sides, then cook at medium heat for 18–25 minutes, according to your taste, turning frequently.

three Meanwhile, add the bleu cheese to the remaining softened butter and blend together until the mixture is smooth.

four Put the shallot and Madeira into a pan, bring to a boil, and boil until reduced to about 2 tablespoons. Stir in the cream, then let simmer for 3 minutes. Add the cheese mixture, a little at a time, whisking after each addition until the sauce is smooth. When all the cheese mixture has been added, remove from the heat. Season to taste with salt and pepper.

five Transfer the cooked tenderloin to a warmed serving dish and let rest for 5 minutes. Slice the tenderloin into steaks and serve with green beans and the Bleu Cheese Sauce drizzled over the top, garnished with chopped parsley. Serve any remaining sauce separately in a pitcher.

cook's tip

You need a semihard bleu cheese for this recipe. Choose from Italian Gorgonzola, French Roquefort, English Stilton, or Danish Blue, depending upon availability and your personal choice.

Cooking steak in a skillet is the ideal way to make use of the meat's cooking juices in a sauce to serve with the steak. And here are some classic examples, such as Beef Stroganoff and Steak Diane, which are perfect for entertaining in that they are both luxurious and easy to prepare.

It is best to use a large, heavy-bottom skillet and preheat it thoroughly before adding a small amount of oil—just enough to prevent the steaks from sticking. Add the steaks to the hot oil and brown them quickly on both sides to seal in the juices before cooking more gently for the remaining time.

pan-fried to perfection

prepare 15 minutes, plus 30 minutes' cooling
cook 5–14 minutes *serves* 4

Steak pan-fried in a skillet until almost black on the outside and rose pink in the middle, accompanied by Béarnaise Sauce, is an authentic French experience and is served in the best restaurants in New York.

pan-fried steaks with béarnaise sauce

ingredients

4 rump, sirloin, or tenderloin steaks, about 6–8 oz/175–225 g each and 1 inch/2.5 cm thick
olive or sunflower-seed oil, for pan-frying
1 tbsp butter, for pan-frying
pepper
fresh watercress sprigs, to garnish

Béarnaise Sauce
4 tbsp white wine or tarragon vinegar
1 shallot, finely chopped
2 fresh tarragon sprigs plus 1 tbsp finely chopped fresh tarragon
2 egg yolks
6 tbsp butter, softened
salt and pepper

To serve
French Fries
Crispy Onion Rings (optional)

one First make the sauce. Put the vinegar, shallot, and tarragon sprigs into a small, heavy-bottom pan over medium-low heat and let simmer until reduced to 1 tablespoon. Let cool.

two Strain the vinegar mixture into a heatproof bowl set over a pan of simmering water. Add the egg yolks and whisk together until thick.

three Gradually add the butter in small pieces, whisking after each addition, until combined and the sauce has thickened. Add the chopped tarragon and season to taste with salt and pepper.

four Cover the surface of the sauce with a piece of dampened waxed paper to prevent a skin from forming. Remove from the heat, but leave over the pan of hot water to keep hot while you cook the steaks.

five Season the steaks to taste with pepper. Heat a film of oil in a large, heavy-bottom skillet over high heat. When hot, add the butter, and as soon as it has melted, add the steaks. Cook quickly on both sides to seal, then reduce the heat to medium and cook, turning once, for 2½–3 minutes each side for rare, 3½–5 minutes each side for medium, and 5–7 minutes each side for well done.

six Transfer the steaks to plates and spoon the sauce over. Garnish with watercress and serve with French Fries and Crispy Onion Rings, if wished.

Perfect for midweek entertaining, this is a dish that can be made in minutes. Serve it with French Fries or mashed potatoes to mop up the creamy mustard sauce.

tenderloin steaks with mustard sauce

ingredients

4 tenderloin steaks, about 6 oz/175 g
  each
2 tbsp butter
1 tbsp olive oil
4 scallions, finely sliced
generous ⅓ cup dry vermouth
1 cup heavy cream or sour cream

1 tbsp whole grain mustard
1 tsp chopped fresh parsley
salt and pepper
arugula leaves, to garnish
French Fries or mashed potatoes,
  to serve (optional)

one Season the steaks to taste with pepper. Melt the butter with the oil in a large, heavy-bottom skillet over high heat. When hot, add the steaks, and cook quickly on both sides to seal. Reduce the heat to medium and cook, turning once, for 2½–3 minutes each side for rare, 3½–5 minutes each side for medium, or 5–7 minutes each side for well done. Season the steaks to taste with salt and pepper, transfer to a warmed serving dish, and keep warm.

two Add the scallions and vermouth to the skillet and cook for 2 minutes, stirring to deglaze by scraping any sediment from the bottom of the skillet. Add the cream and bring to a boil, stirring constantly. Remove the sauce from the heat and stir in the mustard and parsley. Season to taste with salt and pepper.

three Pour the sauce over the steaks and serve at once with French Fries or mashed potato, if wished, and garnished with arugula leaves.

cook's tips

Vermouth is a fortified wine flavored by an infusion of herbs. Although it has more character than wine, white wine could be used as an alternative. Don't be tempted to add the mustard before you have removed the sauce from the heat, as it can separate if overheated.

This is an adaptation of the classic Steak au Poivre, which is served with a sauce containing cream. If wished, you could add about ⅔ cup of heavy cream to the reduced pan juices at the final stage to mellow the fiery peppercorns.

peppered t-bone steaks

ingredients

2 tbsp whole black peppercorns, green peppercorns, or a mixture of both	1 tbsp olive or sunflower-seed oil
	½ cup red wine
2 T-bone steaks, about 9 oz/250 g each	salt
2 tbsp butter	freshly cooked vegetables, to serve

one Put the peppercorns into a mortar and coarsely crush with a pestle, or put into a strong plastic bag, place on a cutting board, and coarsely crush with the end of a rolling pin.

two Spread the crushed peppercorns out on a plate and press one side of each steak hard into them to encrust the surface of the meat. Turn over and repeat with the other side.

three Melt the butter with the oil in a large, heavy-bottom skillet over high heat. When hot, add the steaks, and cook quickly on both sides to seal. Reduce the heat to medium and cook, turning once, for 2½–3 minutes each side for rare, 3½–5 minutes each side for medium, or 5–7 minutes each side for well done. Transfer the steaks to warmed plates and keep warm.

four Add the wine to the skillet and stir to deglaze by scraping any sediment from the bottom of the skillet. Bring to a boil and boil until reduced by about half. Season to taste with salt. Pour the pan juices over the steaks and serve at once with freshly cooked vegetables.

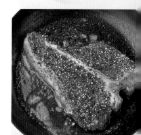

did you know?

It is mainly Texas that supplies America with huge T-bone steaks. On one side of the bone is the sirloin, with its strip of fat running along the edge, and on the other side is the fillet. It is a juicy cut with a good flavor and is suitable for pan-frying, broiling, or grilling —and will satisfy anyone with a large appetite!

Steak, coated in egg and bread crumbs, pan-fried like chicken until crispy, and served with onion sauce, is a good, filling family meal. This is especially true when served, as it traditionally is, with mashed potatoes.

chicken-fried steaks

ingredients

1 piece of rump steak, about 1 lb 2 oz/
   500 g, or 4 thin frying steaks
1 egg, beaten
1 tbsp plus 1 cup milk
⅞ cup dried white bread crumbs
vegetable oil, for pan-frying
1 onion, thinly sliced

2 tbsp all-purpose flour
salt and pepper
fresh thyme sprigs, to garnish

To serve
mashed potatoes
hot pepper sauce (optional)

one If using rump steak, trim the fat. Using a meat mallet or heavy wooden rolling pin, pound the steak on a wooden board until it is ¼ inch/5 mm thick. Cut the steak into 4 equal-size pieces.

two Beat the egg and the 1 tablespoon of milk together on a large, deep plate or in a soup bowl and season to taste with salt and pepper. Spread the bread crumbs out on a separate large plate. Dip the steaks into the egg mixture, shaking off any surplus, then coat in the bread crumbs. Let rest on another large plate for 2–3 minutes.

three Meanwhile, heat ¼ inch/5 mm of oil in a large, heavy-bottom skillet over medium-high heat. (You may have to cook the steaks in 2 batches if your skillet is not large enough to hold the steaks in a single layer.) When the oil is hot, carefully add the steaks and cook for 3 minutes on each side until golden brown and crisp, turning once. Transfer the steaks to a warmed serving dish and keep warm.

four Pour off all but 2–3 tablespoons of the oil in the skillet. Return to the heat, add the onion, and cook, stirring frequently, for 5 minutes until softened. Add the flour and cook for 1 minute, stirring constantly. Remove from the heat and, using a wooden spoon, gradually stir in the 1 cup of milk until smooth, scraping any sediment from the bottom of the skillet. Return to the heat and slowly bring to a boil, stirring constantly, until the sauce thickens. Season to taste with salt and pepper.

five Pour the onion sauce over the steaks, garnish with thyme, and serve at once with mashed potatoes and hot pepper sauce, if wished.

Thick rib-eye steaks have a little more fat than other steaks, but they're full of flavor and, combined with mushrooms, make a scrumptious dish. That said, you could use rump or sirloin steaks instead if preferred.

rib-eye steaks
with mushrooms

ingredients

3 tbsp butter
1 tbsp olive or sunflower-seed oil
4 boneless rib-eye steaks, about
 8 oz/225 g each
1 garlic clove, finely chopped

8 oz/225 g white mushrooms, halved or
 quartered
4 tbsp Madeira or port
salt and pepper
chopped fresh parsley, to garnish
freshly cooked vegetables, to serve

one Melt the butter with the oil in a large, heavy-bottom skillet over a high heat. When hot, add the steaks, and cook quickly on both sides to seal. Reduce the heat to medium and cook, turning once, for 2½–3 minutes each side for rare, 3½–5 minutes each side for medium, or 5–7 minutes each side for well done. Transfer the steaks to warmed plates and keep warm.

two Add the garlic and mushrooms to the skillet and cook, stirring frequently, for 5 minutes, or until softened. Add the Madeira and stir the mixture to deglaze by scraping any sediment from the bottom of the skillet. Season to taste with salt and pepper.

three Spoon the mushrooms and pan juices over the steaks and serve at once with freshly cooked vegetables, garnished with chopped parsley.

variations
Noisettes of lamb can be prepared in the same way, when the dish is known as Médicis. It is traditionally served with new potatoes and artichoke hearts tossed in butter, together with peas and small balls of carrots and turnips arranged alternately, as a garnish. You could serve the steaks in the same way.

prepare 10 minutes, plus 2 hours' freezing
cook 10–12 minutes *serves* 4

This rich dish has always been popular for entertaining. Use the tail end of a beef tenderloin to keep the cost down or use rump steak as an alternative. Serve with buttered noodles or rice and a green salad.

beef stroganoff

ingredients

1 beef tenderloin, about 1 lb 8 oz/675 g, frozen for 2 hours
4 tbsp butter
1 tbsp olive or sunflower-seed oil
1 onion, thinly sliced
8 oz/225 g white or shiitake mushrooms, thinly sliced
1 tsp French mustard

1¼ cups sour cream
salt and pepper
fresh parsley sprigs and chopped fresh parsley, to garnish

To serve
rice or noodles
green salad

one Thinly slice the partially frozen steak across the grain into bite-size strips. Season to taste with pepper.

two Melt the butter with the oil in a large, heavy-bottom skillet or ovenproof casserole over medium heat. Add the onion and cook for 5 minutes, or until softened and beginning to brown.

three Add the mushrooms and cook for 2–3 minutes, stirring frequently, until lightly browned. Using a slotted spoon, transfer the onion and mushrooms to a plate.

four Add the steak strips to the skillet and cook, stirring frequently, for 2–3 minutes until browned on the outside but still pink inside. Return the onion and mushrooms and any juices to the skillet and toss together.

five Stir the mustard into the sour cream, then stir into the skillet. Heat gently without boiling, stirring constantly. Season to taste with salt and pepper and serve at once with rice or noodles and a green salad, garnished with fresh parsley.

did you know?

It is thought that this dish was created in the 18th century by the French chef of the Russian nobleman Count Stroganoff. Having to prepare a meal quickly from some beef that had frozen due to the Siberian weather, he found that if he sliced it very thinly, he didn't have to defrost it—a tip worth remembering!

It is to Chinatown that New Yorkers go for the best Chinese food. Fortunately, stir-fried dishes, cooked in a single pan, are quick and simple to prepare at home, as this recipe proves.

stir-fried steak and broccoli with noodles

ingredients

1 piece of sirloin, rump, or boneless rib-eye steak, about 9 oz/250 g

5½ oz/150 g small broccoli florets

3½ oz/100 g baby corn

3 tbsp vegetable oil

1 garlic clove, thinly sliced

1 tsp grated fresh gingerroot

4 scallions, thinly sliced

2 tbsp oyster sauce

10½ oz/300 g straight-to-wok thread noodles

splash of soy sauce (optional)

pepper

cilantro sprigs, to garnish

one If possible, partially freeze the steak for about 2 hours to make it easier to slice. Slice the steak, across the grain, as thinly as possible. Cut each broccoli floret into quarters and cut the corn in half lengthwise.

two Heat a wok or large, heavy-bottom skillet over high heat until hot. Add ½ tablespoon of the oil and swirl it around to coat the wok. Add the steak slices and stir-fry for 2 minutes until browned on all sides. Using a slotted spoon, transfer the steak to a warmed plate and set aside.

three Add the remaining oil to the wok and, when hot, add the garlic, ginger, and broccoli and stir-fry for 2 minutes. Add the corn and scallions and stir-fry for 1 minute.

four Return the steak and juices to the wok and toss together. Add the oyster sauce and stir-fry for 1 minute. Add the noodles and stir-fry for a final 1–2 minutes until they are heated through. Season to taste with pepper and add the soy sauce, if wished. Serve at once, garnished with cilantro sprigs.

cook's tip

Instead of using precooked noodles, you could use dried thread or medium egg noodles. Simply cook in boiling water as directed on the package, drain, and rinse under cold water, then drain again. Incidentally, in China, noodles are regarded as a symbol of long life.

Pan-fried steak and onions go hand in hand, and in this recipe the onions are cooked almost to a purée, which, with the addition of cream and wine, provides a delicious sauce for serving with steak on a special occasion.

minute steaks
with onion sauce

ingredients

5 tbsp butter

2 tbsp vegetable oil

1 lb/450 g onions, thinly sliced

scant 1 cup red wine

4 minute or frying steaks

⅔ cup heavy cream

salt and pepper

green salad, to serve

one Melt 3 tablespoons of the butter with half the oil in a large pan over medium heat. Add the onions, cover, and cook, stirring occasionally, for 10–15 minutes until softened and light golden brown.

two Add half the wine to the onions and season to taste with salt and pepper. Bring to a boil, then reduce the heat to low and cook for an additional 5–10 minutes until very soft.

three Meanwhile, melt the remaining butter with the remaining oil in a large, heavy-bottom skillet over medium heat. When hot, add the steaks, and cook, turning once, for 30–45 seconds each side for rare or 1–1½ minutes each side for medium. Season to taste with salt and pepper.

four Strain the cooked onions, reserving the liquid, and place in a warmed serving dish. Arrange the cooked steaks on top.

five Add the remaining wine to the skillet in which the steaks were cooked and bring to a boil, stirring to deglaze by scraping any sediment from the bottom of the skillet. Stir in the reserved onion liquid and the cream and season to taste with salt and pepper. Return to a boil, then reduce the heat and let simmer for 1–2 minutes.

six Spoon a little of the sauce over the steaks and serve with the remaining sauce separately in a pitcher and a green salad.

cook's tip

Minute or frying steaks are lean, thinly sliced steaks, which are inexpensive and are best if cooked quickly. They are more suitable for pan-frying than broiling, which tends to dry them out, and if overcooked they have a tendency to become tough.

Succulent tenderloin steaks cooked in brandy is a classic dish served in top New York restaurants. Fortunately, it can easily be prepared at home and needs only new potatoes, tossed in butter and chopped parsley, and a green salad to accompany it.

steak diane

ingredients

2 tenderloin steaks, about 6 oz/175 g
  each
2½ tbsp butter
1 tbsp olive or sunflower-seed oil
1 shallot, finely chopped
2 tbsp brandy
1 tsp Worcestershire sauce
2 tsp lemon juice

3 tbsp Homemade Tomato Sauce
1½ tbsp chopped fresh parsley
salt and pepper

To serve
freshly cooked new potatoes
green salad

one Using a meat mallet or heavy wooden rolling pin, pound the steaks on a wooden board until they are ¼ inch/5 mm thick. Season to taste with pepper.

two Melt 2 tablespoons of the butter with the oil in a large, heavy-bottom skillet over medium heat, add the shallot, and cook for 2–3 minutes until softened. Push the shallot to the side of the skillet.

three Add the steaks to the skillet and cook for 1–2 minutes on each side until browned. Pour the brandy over the steaks, remove from the heat, and ignite the pan juices.

four When the flames have died down, stir the Worcestershire sauce, lemon juice, and Homemade Tomato Sauce into the pan juices. Heat gently, stir in 1 tablespoon of the parsley, and season to taste with salt and pepper. Serve at once with new potatoes tossed in the remaining butter and parsley, and a green salad.

did you know?

This well-known dish originated in Australia, where it was created by a restaurant chef. In restaurants there, and in America, it is often cooked in front of you, at the table—the spectacle of flambéed steaks is impressive!

prepare 10 minutes, plus 4 hours' marinating
cook 20–30 minutes *serves* 4

First the steaks are marinated to impart flavor and make them tender, then they are pan-fried and coated in a sauce rich in barbecue flavors for a melt-in-the-mouth result.

steaks in barbecue sauce

ingredients

3 tbsp vegetable oil
2 tbsp red wine vinegar
1 garlic clove, crushed
2 tbsp Worcestershire sauce
1 tbsp tomato paste
1 tbsp mustard powder
4 boneless rib-eye, rump, or sirloin
   steaks, about 6–8 oz/175–225 g each

1 large onion, thinly sliced
14 oz/400 g canned chopped tomatoes
1 tbsp soft brown sugar
few drops of hot pepper sauce
salt and pepper
fresh green salad, to serve (optional)

one To make the marinade, put 1 tablespoon of the oil, the vinegar, garlic, Worcestershire sauce, tomato paste, mustard powder, and salt and pepper to taste into a large, shallow, nonmetallic dish large enough to hold the steaks in a single layer, and mix together. Add the steaks and turn in the marinade to coat them. Cover and let marinate in the refrigerator for at least 4 hours or up to 24 hours, turning occasionally.

two When ready to cook, heat the remaining oil in a large, heavy-bottom skillet or ovenproof casserole over medium heat. Add the onion and cook, stirring occasionally, for 10 minutes until softened and golden brown. Push the onion to one side of the skillet.

three Increase the heat to high. Using a slotted spoon, remove the steaks from the marinade, reserving the marinade, add the steaks to the skillet, and cook quickly on both sides to seal. Reduce the heat to medium and cook, turning once, for 2½–3 minutes each side for rare, 3½–5 minutes each side for medium, or 5–7 minutes each side for well done. Transfer the steaks to a warmed dish and keep warm.

four Add the tomatoes with their juice, the sugar, and reserved marinade to the skillet and stir to deglaze by scraping any sediment from the bottom of the skillet and incorporating the onions. Bring to a boil, then reduce the heat and let simmer for 2–3 minutes. Add the hot pepper sauce and salt and pepper to taste.

five Return the steaks to the skillet and baste with the sauce. Serve at once with a fresh green salad, if wished.

It is those little extras that can make all the difference to a dish. A plainly grilled or broiled steak, for instance, wouldn't be the same without a crowning slice of melting Savory Butter. Where would a burger be without a decent dollop of Homemade Tomato Sauce? A perfectly pan-fried, moist steak, served with French Fries to absorb the delicious juices, is the one occasion where you can forget about having to serve the meat with something green. And then there are the definitive examples of the sweet-and-sour relishes and fresh and fiery salsas for which America is famed, and deservedly so, to provide the perfect piquant finishing touch.

finishing touches

Tomato ketchup has its place, but nothing compares with this homemade sauce, served with freshly cooked pan-fried, broiled, or grilled steak.

homemade tomato sauce

ingredients

1 tbsp butter

2 tbsp olive oil

1 onion, chopped

1 garlic clove, finely chopped

14 oz/400 g canned tomatoes or
  1 lb/450 g fresh tomatoes, peeled

1 tbsp tomato paste

generous ⅓ cup red wine

⅔ cup vegetable stock

½ tsp sugar

1 bay leaf

salt and pepper

one Melt the butter with the oil in a large pan over medium heat, add the onion and garlic, and cook, stirring frequently, for 5 minutes, or until the onion has softened and is beginning to brown.

two Add all the remaining ingredients to the pan and season to taste with salt and pepper. Bring to a boil, then reduce the heat to low and let simmer, uncovered and stirring occasionally, for 30 minutes, or until the tomato sauce has thickened.

three Remove and discard the bay leaf, pour the sauce into a food processor or blender, and process until smooth. Alternatively, using the back of a wooden spoon, push the sauce through a nylon strainer into a bowl.

four If serving at once, reheat the sauce gently in a pan. Alternatively, store and reheat before serving.

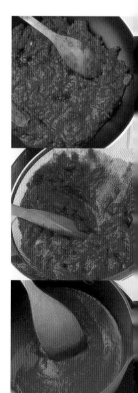

cook's tip

The sauce can be stored in an airtight container in the refrigerator for up to 4–5 days, or alternatively, you can store it in the freezer.

These onions are coated in a thick batter and deep-fried until crisp and golden brown, but for a lighter alternative, simply dip them in milk followed by seasoned flour before deep-frying.

crispy onion rings

ingredients

generous ¾ cup all-purpose flour
1 egg
⅔ cup lowfat milk
4 large onions

vegetable oil, for deep-frying
chili powder, to taste (optional)
salt and pepper
lettuce leaves, to serve

one To make the batter, put the flour and a pinch of salt into a large bowl and make a well in the center. Break the egg into the well and gently beat with a whisk. Gradually whisk in the milk, drawing the flour from the side into the liquid in the center to form a smooth batter.

two Leaving the onions whole, slice widthwise into ¼-inch/5-mm slices, then separate each slice into rings.

three Heat the oil in a deep-fryer or deep, heavy-bottom pan to 350–375°F/180–190°C, or until a cube of bread browns in 30 seconds.

four Using the tines of a fork, pick up several onion rings at a time and dip in the batter. Let any excess batter drip off, then add the onions to the oil and deep-fry for 1–2 minutes until they rise to the surface of the oil and become crisp and golden brown. Remove from the oil, drain on paper towels, and keep warm while deep-frying the remaining onion rings in batches. Do not try to deep-fry too many at a time, as this will reduce the temperature of the oil and the onion rings will absorb some of the oil and become soggy.

five Season the onion rings with chili powder, if wished, and salt and pepper to taste and serve at once on a bed of lettuce leaves.

cook's tip

There are dozens of different methods that people claim can help to prevent you from crying while cutting onions, such as leaving the root intact until the very end, peeling them under running water, chilling them before cutting, and even whistling while you work!

prepare 10 minutes, plus 2 hours' cooling
cook 15 minutes *serves* 6–8

This is a relish to rustle up quickly. Made in a small quantity, you only need to wait for it to cool before serving, rather than preserving it and letting it mature.

roasted bell pepper relish

ingredients

1 red bell pepper
1 yellow bell pepper
1 green bell pepper
1 tbsp extra virgin olive oil

½ tsp brown sugar
1 tsp balsamic vinegar
¼ tsp salt
¼ tsp paprika

one Preheat the broiler to medium. Put the bell peppers onto a broiler rack and cook, turning frequently, for 15 minutes, or until the skins are charred all over.

two Transfer the bell peppers to a bowl, then immediately cover with a clean, damp dish towel and leave for at least 2 hours, or overnight, until cold.

three When the bell peppers are cold, hold them over a clean bowl to collect the juices and peel off the skin. Remove and discard the stem, core, and seeds and finely dice the flesh.

four Add the diced bell peppers to the juices in the bowl, then add the oil, sugar, vinegar, salt, and paprika. Stir together until well mixed, and serve, or store in an airtight container in the refrigerator for up to 4–5 days.

cook's tip

The recipe uses a selection of different colored bell peppers, but this isn't essential—it just makes the preserve look more colorful. So you could use all of one color or two colors if preferred.

prepare 15 minutes
cook 1 hour 50 minutes *serves* 4

Instead of serving these sweet, caramelized onions as a hot vegetable accompaniment, you can serve them as a condiment with broiled, grilled, or pan-fried steak, burgers, or cold cooked meats.

sweet-and-sour glazed onions

ingredients

1 lb 8 oz/675 g pearl or pickling onions	1 tbsp tomato paste
4 tbsp butter	2 tbsp sugar
1 tbsp olive oil	2 tbsp red wine vinegar
1½ cups water	salt and pepper

one Peel the onions, but keep the root intact so that they do not fall apart during cooking. Melt the butter with the oil in a large, heavy-bottom skillet over medium heat, add the onions, and cook for 5 minutes, gently shaking the skillet occasionally.

two Add the water and tomato paste to the skillet and cook for 30 minutes, stirring frequently.

three Add the sugar and vinegar to the onions and season to taste with salt and pepper. Reduce the heat to low and cook for 1¼ hours, or until tender and golden brown. If the mixture shows signs of becoming too dry, add a little more water. Serve hot or cold.

serving recommendation

If being served hot as a vegetable accompaniment, 2 tablespoons of raisins or golden raisins can be added about 30 minutes before the end of cooking. If being served cold as a condiment, the onions can be prepared ahead and stored in the refrigerator for several days.

No plain broiled or grilled steak would be complete without a slice of Savory Butter gently melting on top. Maître d'Hôtel Butter, with its parsley and lemon juice, is the traditional accompaniment, but all the recipes here make excellent finishing touches.

savory butters

ingredients

½ cup butter
salt and pepper

Maître d'Hôtel Butter
3 tbsp finely chopped fresh parsley
1 tbsp lemon juice

Mustard Butter
2 tbsp French, whole grain, Dijon, or
  herb mustard

Garlic Butter
2 garlic cloves, crushed
2 tsp finely chopped fresh parsley

Horseradish Butter
2 tbsp creamed horseradish

one Put the butter into a bowl and beat with a wooden spoon until softened. Add the ingredients for your choice of Savory Butter, season to taste with salt and pepper, and blend together until well mixed.

two Turn the mixture out onto a sheet of waxed paper and shape into a roll. Wrap in the waxed paper and let chill in the refrigerator for 2–3 hours until firm. Just before serving, slice into thin circles.

cook's tip
These butters can be made well in advance so that you have them to hand at a moment's notice. They can be stored in the refrigerator for up to 4–5 days or can be wrapped in foil and stored in the freezer until required.

prepare 15 minutes, plus 15 minutes' draining
cook about 25 minutes serves 3–4

Recipes for Hashed Brown Potatoes vary greatly from region to region. They might use grated raw, cubed raw, or cooked potatoes, but whichever you use, there is no comparison between a homecooked and a store-bought, frozen variety!

hashed brown potatoes

ingredients

4 large potatoes
1 small onion, finely chopped (optional)
1 tbsp butter

vegetable oil, for pan-frying
salt and pepper
fresh parsley sprigs, to garnish

one Peel, then coarsely grate the potatoes. Put into a strainer and rinse under cold running water, then let drain for about 15 minutes. Using the back of a wooden spoon, push out any excess water, then wrap the potatoes in a clean dish towel and dry very thoroughly.

two Put the potatoes into a large bowl. Add the onion, if using, season to taste with salt and pepper and mix well together.

three Melt the butter with a generous film of oil in a large, heavy-bottom skillet over medium heat. When hot, add the potatoes and toss them several times in the butter and oil, then press down with a spatula and spread evenly over the bottom of the skillet. Press down firmly again. Reduce the heat to low, cover, and cook for 10 minutes, or until the base of the pancake is crisp and golden brown. During cooking, press the pancake down several more times and gently shake the skillet to make sure it isn't sticking.

four Using a spatula, cut the pancake into 4 wedges, then carefully turn each wedge. If the bottom of the skillet appears too dry, add a little more oil to prevent the potatoes from sticking. Cook the second side, uncovered, for 15 minutes, or until tender and golden brown. Serve at once.

variation

The potatoes in this recipe are cooked as one large, round pancake, but if preferred, they can be cooked as individual pancakes in the same way.

Potato wedges are a contemporary way of serving potatoes.
Here they are spiced, according to your taste, for serving as an
accompaniment, but they are equally good served as a snack
(see Serving Recommendation).

spicy potato wedges

ingredients

1 lb 8 oz/675 g large, firm potatoes, such
  as round white, round red, Yukon gold,
  or russet
3 tbsp vegetable oil

1 tbsp paprika or 2 tsp ground
  coriander, 1 tsp cumin seeds,
  and 1 tsp turmeric
salt and pepper
chopped cilantro leaves, to garnish

one Preheat the oven to 400°F/200°C. Peel the potatoes, then cut each in
half lengthwise and then in half again until you have 8 even-shaped wedges.
Put into a large pan of salted water, bring to a boil, and boil for 3 minutes.
Drain well and return the wedges to the pan.

two Add the oil to the pan and toss the potato wedges in it until coated.
Add the paprika or ground coriander, cumin seeds, and turmeric, season to
taste with salt and pepper, and mix well together.

three Spread the potato wedges out on a baking sheet and bake in the
oven for 35–40 minutes until tender and golden brown, turning 2–3 times
during cooking. Serve hot, sprinkled with chopped cilantro to garnish.

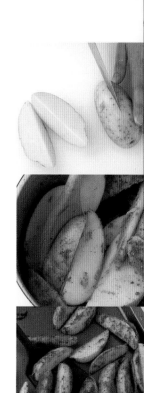

serving recommendation
To serve as a snack, sprinkle the cooked potato wedges
with grated cheese, cook them under a preheated
medium broiler until the cheese is melted and bubbling,
and serve with a dip such as Tomato Salsa or one of the
Steak Dipping Sauces, or simply with a bowl of sour
cream and chives.

A fiery salsa beautifully complements a plainly cooked steak, as well as dishes of Mexican origin adopted by America, such as the Chili con Carne Burritos and Steak and Lime Tortillas.

tomato salsa

ingredients

1 lb/450 g firm, ripe tomatoes

1 fresh jalapeño or other small hot chili pepper

2 tsp extra virgin olive oil

1 garlic clove, crushed

grated rind and juice of 1 lime

pinch of sugar

4 tbsp chopped cilantro

salt

cilantro sprigs, to garnish

one Using a sharp knife, finely dice the tomatoes and put into a bowl with the seeds. Halve the chili, remove and discard the seeds, and very finely dice the flesh. Add to the tomatoes.

two Add all the remaining ingredients to the tomatoes, season to taste with salt, and mix well together.

three Turn the mixture into a small, nonmetallic serving bowl, cover, and leave at room temperature for 30 minutes to let the flavors combine. If not being served straight away, the salsa can be stored in the refrigerator for up to 2–3 days, but it is best if allowed to return to room temperature for 1 hour before being served. Serve garnished with cilantro sprigs.

did you know?

Literally translated from Italian and Spanish, salsa means sauce and can refer to anything from a white sauce to a barbecue sauce. However, when we use the word salsa, we tend to think of the tomato and chili sauces that are made from raw, fresh vegetables and are served cold as an accompaniment.

Horseradish and mustard are seasonings that were made for steak, and here they are used to create two delicious dipping sauces, along with a rich bleu cheese variation. These kinds of dipping sauces are to be found in restaurants serving steak in many regions of America.

steak dipping sauces

ingredients

1 cup sour cream
salt and pepper
fresh dill sprigs or chives, to garnish

Horseradish Dipping Sauce
3 tbsp grated horseradish
1 tsp chopped fresh dill

Mustard Dipping Sauce
1 tbsp French, Dijon, or whole grain mustard
1 tbsp chopped fresh parsley or snipped fresh chives

Bleu Cheese Dipping Sauce
1 oz/25 g bleu cheese, such as Gorgonzola, Roquefort, or Stilton, crumbled
1 garlic clove, crushed

one Put the sour cream into a bowl. Add the ingredients for your choice of Dipping Sauce, season to taste with salt and pepper, and blend together until well mixed.

two Turn the mixture into a small serving bowl, cover, and let chill in the refrigerator for 30 minutes before serving or until required. Serve garnished with fresh dill sprigs or chives.

serving recommendation
You can serve these dipping sauces for a steak fondue or as sauces with broiled, grilled, or fried steak. They are also good served with bread-crumbed chicken pieces or drizzled over a mixed vegetable salad.

prepare 10 minutes, plus about 50 minutes' soaking and cooling
cook 25–35 minutes serves 4

French fries, pommes frites, or chips, from chunky to shoestring—
call them what you wish, but a simply broiled, grilled, or pan-fried
steak wouldn't be the same without this classic bistro accompaniment!

french fries

ingredients

1 lb 8 oz/675 g large potatoes
(see Cook's Tip)

sunflower-seed, corn, or peanut oil, for
deep-frying
salt and pepper

one Peel the potatoes and cut into ⅜-inch/8-mm even-size fingers. As soon
as they are prepared, put them into a large bowl of cold water to prevent
discoloration, then let them soak for 30 minutes to remove the excess starch.

two Drain the potatoes and dry well on a clean dish towel. Heat the oil in a
deep-fryer or large, heavy-bottom pan to 375°F/190°C. If you do not have
a thermometer, test the temperature by dropping a potato finger into the oil.
If it sinks, the oil isn't hot enough; if it floats and the oil bubbles around it,
it is ready. Carefully add a small batch of potatoes to the oil (this is to ensure
even cooking and to avoid reducing the temperature of the oil) and deep-fry
for 5–6 minutes until soft but not browned. Remove from the oil and drain
well on paper towels. Let cool for at least 5 minutes. Continue to deep-fry the
remaining potatoes in the same way, allowing the oil to return to the correct
temperature each time.

three When ready to serve, reheat the oil to 400°F/200°C. Add the
potatoes, in small batches, and deep-fry for 2–3 minutes until golden brown.
Remove from the oil and drain on paper towels. Serve at once, seasoned to
taste with salt and pepper.

cook's tip

*The secret of making crisp, golden fries is to cook the
potatoes in small batches, in two stages—in advance
and just before serving—and to use a variety of potato
that produces a crisp outer shell with a fluffy, light
inside. Russet Burbank, Russet Arcadia, California long
whites, or Butte are all suitable.*

index